Developing literacy Skills

Spelling

KEY STAGE 2: Y5–6/ P6–7

RAY BARKER
AND
GLEN FRANKLIN

HOPSCOTCH
EDUCATIONAL PUBLISHING

Contents

Published by Hopscotch Educational Publishing Company Ltd, 8 Severn Close, Leamington Spa CV32 7BZ.

© 1998 Hopscotch Educational Publishing

Written by Ray Barker and Glen Franklin
Series design by Blade Communications
Illustrated by Pat Murray
Cover illustration by Pat Murray
Printed by Clintplan, Southam

Ray Barker and Glen Franklin hereby assert their moral right to be identified as the authors of this work in accordance with the Copyright, Designs and Patents Act, 1988.

ISBN 1-902239-08-3

Introduction

◆ ABOUT THE SERIES ◆

Developing Literacy Skills is a series of books aimed at developing key literacy skills using stories, non-fiction, poetry and rhyme, spelling and grammar, from Key Stage 1 (P1–3) through to Key Stage 2 (P4–7).

The series offers a structured approach which provides detailed lesson plans to teach specific literacy skills. A unique feature of the series is the provision of differentiated photocopiable activities aimed at considerably reducing teacher preparation time. Suggestions for using the photocopiable pages as a stimulus for further work in the classroom is provided to ensure maximum use of this resource.

◆ ABOUT THIS BOOK ◆

There is no one way to teach spelling. Good teachers use a variety of methods to give children a sense of pattern in language and the many exceptions to the rules that are found. What is clear is that structure and practice are both necessary. Children do not learn spelling skills through osmosis. The activities in this book develop through a phonological approach – but they are not slaves to phonics. The differentiated activities involve children in:
- ✦ investigating patterns and collecting examples of words
- ✦ reading and spelling words
- ✦ generating and practising new words

The activities are not meant to be followed in sequential order, and many of them are generic in that they can be developed and used in many different situations.

In English, spelling is a very difficult skill to learn. Rules can be taught and understood, but they only take children so far, as the poem on page 64 illustrates so delightfully. Investigating sound patterns and playing with language through regular, concentrated and challenging practice can help them to understand the peculiarities of spelling.

◆ CHAPTER CONTENT ◆

✦ Overall aims

These outline the aims for both lessons.

✦ Teacher information

This provides background knowledge on the content of the lesson.

✦ Intended learning

This sets out the specific objectives for each lesson.

✦ Starting point

This provides ideas for introducing the activity.

✦ Activity

This explains the task(s) the children will carry out in the lesson without supporting photocopiable activities.

✦ Using the differentiated activity sheets

How to use each sheet and guidance on the type of child who will benefit most from each sheet.

✦ Plenary session

This suggests ideas for whole-class sessions to discuss the learning outcomes and follow-up work.

✦ Using the photocopiable sheets as a stimulus for further work

This is a useful list of further activities that can be developed from the activity sheets.

✦ Other ideas for using . . .

This contains other ideas for developing the skill being addressed in this chapter.

Word families and common roots

◆ Overall aims

- ◆ To collect and classify words with common roots.
- ◆ To recognise and investigate spelling patterns in word families.
- ◆ To read and spell words with common roots and generate new words by analogy.

◆ Teacher information

- ◆ Recognising and learning component parts of words is a useful aid to spelling. Knowing the relationships between words and identifying recurring patterns enables children to formulate and generate a wider range of words, through making links between known and unknown parts.
- ◆ Historically, the English spelling system has borrowed and retained words from many different sources. Exploration of these common roots can lead to a greater understanding. This is particularly helpful to speakers of languages other than English, who may recognise roots from other sources.
- ◆ The activities in this chapter may generate lots of new and unfamiliar vocabulary. It is important to encourage the use of dictionaries to establish understanding and to put words in context.
- ◆ The most important issue in all these activities is that children should sound out the words and hear the sound they are making.

◆ LESSON ONE ◆

◆ Intended learning

- ◆ To collect and classify words with common roots.

◆ Starting point: Whole class

- ◆ Begin by reminding the children of the metalanguage encountered previously, and reinforce understanding of syllables, prefixes and suffixes where required, and referring to class word banks.

- ◆ Write a common root on the board, such as *part*. Ask the children to read the word aloud and identify that it has only one syllable. Prompt them to contribute other words they know that include this syllable. List the words given, for example *party*, *depart*, *particle*, and circle the common root in each word.
- ◆ Repeat the activity, using a root that is not an identifiable word, such as *dict* as in *dictionary*. Again, list the words that have the same root – *predict*, *dictation*. In discussion, identify the parts of the word, for example if a known prefix such as *pre*, or a suffix such as *tion* has been added.

◆ Group activities

Explain that the children will be exploring common roots, and making their own collections of words. Encourage collaboration between the groups, as they search for word families, so that the work becomes a whole-class task.

- ◆ Give each group a common root, such as *cent*, *vent*, *play*, *cord*, *sign* and *press*. Using known books, dictionary sources and word banks, ask them to collect as many words as possible that contain their root. Point out that they must find a way to sort and classify their words to explain to the rest of the class.

◆ Plenary session

Ask each group to explain their classifications, noting identification of prefixes and suffixes, syllabic parts, whether the root changes its spelling (*admit* but *admission*) and the position of the root in the word. Explore the word meanings and ask the children to predict from existing knowledge what the root might mean, such as *cent* for 100. As a closing activity, from the lists of words collected, provide a definition and ask the children to identify the word and give its root. For example, "It's a living thing and people say it has one hundred legs." The children give the word *centipede* and the root *cent*.

 **LESSON TWO**

 ## Intended learning

- ◆ To recognise and investigate spelling patterns in word families.
- ◆ To read and spell words with common roots and generate new words by analogy.

 ## Starting Point: Whole class

- ◆ Revise the work from the previous lesson, reminding the children what they discovered about common roots and word families, and referring back to the collections they made.

 ## Using the differentiated activity sheets

Explain to the children that they are going to continue looking at common roots and that they will be collecting and writing new words of their own.

Activity sheet 1

This is aimed at children who can recognise and sort words with common roots into families, but would have difficulty in generating their own words unaided.

Activity sheet 2

This is aimed at children who can recognise and sort words with common roots into families, and can follow examples to generate their own words.

Activity sheet 3

This is aimed at children who can recognise parts of words and use these to generate and classify words, and build new ones of their own by analogy.

 ## Plenary session

After the children have completed their tasks, bring the whole class together to share and discuss the work. The teacher can use this time to assess the understanding of each group, by prompting questions using the lists the children have collected and classified.

For Activity sheet 1

Provide a collection of words on cards and ask the children to sort the words, read them and identify the common root. Ask them to give you another word with the same root.

For Activity sheet 2

Use the same words from the Photocopiable Sheet, mounted on card. Ask the child to re-sort the words and identify the common roots. Prompt the child with another word from one of the word families and ask "Can you write the root for me? Can you now write the whole word?"

For Activity sheet 3

Provide a variety of syllables and roots of words. Ask the child to make a known word from the parts. Remove the parts and ask the child to generate a new word using the same root.

As a closing activity, play Chain Roots. One child stands up and writes a starter word on the board, such as *century*. The class call out other words in the same family – *centigrade*, *centurion*. These are also listed on the board by the first child, helped with spelling by other children and the teacher if required. When the chain is broken, the child counts up how many words the class was able to generate. This score is then recorded. Can it be beaten next time? Will another starter word yield a higher score?

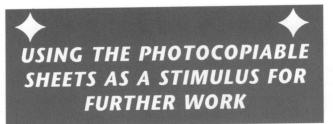

USING THE PHOTOCOPIABLE SHEETS AS A STIMULUS FOR FURTHER WORK

◆ Activity sheet 1

- ✦ Play Root Bingo. Each child is given a baseboard with a collection of common roots. Words are written on small cards, and the children take it in turns to choose a card and place it on the baseboard if appropriate.
- ✦ Devise mnemonics as an aide-memoire to learning the spellings of word families.

◆ Activity sheet 2

- ✦ Set a Syllable Challenge. Taking a common root, such as *rest*, try and find the word with most syllables, *interesting* has 4, *disinterested* has 5!
- ✦ Investigate the crossword facility on some Spellcheckers and word processors, to generate new words.
- ✦ Choose a common root and write a short story or rhyme which uses as many words as possible from that word family.

◆ Activity sheet 3

- ✦ Devise dictionaries for common roots, exploring the word meanings and looking for similarities and differences in any rules that apply.
- ✦ Play Root Links. Provide a collection of words, from a number of different word families. Play is similar to dominoes, in that a card is laid down if a link can be established with the starter card.
- ✦ Play What Is It? Provide a collection of definitions from word families. The children take turns to choose a definition, identify the root and then write the word. Another player checks the spelling, using a spellchecker or dictionary. A challenge could be introduced, with another player electing to attempt the word, but with a forfeit if they make a mistake!

OTHER IDEAS FOR WORD FAMILIES AND COMMON ROOTS

- ✦ Begin to investigate the origins of the roots – *cent* from the Latin meaning 100, *dict* from the Latin word meaning to say.
- ✦ Look for exceptions, for example *decent* derives from a different Latin word meaning to be fitting.
- ✦ Use magazines and newspaper articles to see how word families can be used for persuasion, such as 'The car with perfect performance'. The children could design their own advertisements or newspaper headlines, using some of the word families they have collected.
- ✦ Encourage bilingual children to investigate words in their own language, and to record these in word banks for class reference.

Generally, encourage the children to use the **Look, Say, Cover, Write, Say, Check** method for learning spellings.

Keep in mind that there is a real relationship between handwriting and spelling.

Writing letter strings in a consistent and regular way helps children to register patterns in a multi-sensory way.

Developing
literacy
Skills

Spelling

◆ Posting the letters ◆

In my postbag I have lots of words. I need to sort them out and put them in the post boxes. Can you help me?

playground

signal

resign   decent   centipede

display   replay   century

signature

The root is _____

The root is _____

The root is _____

◆ Match the pairs ◆

◆ Draw lines to join the pairs of words. Draw a circle around the common root.

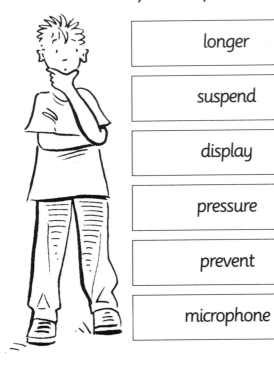

longer	depress
suspend	adventure
display	belong
pressure	phoneme
prevent	discuss
microphone	pendulum

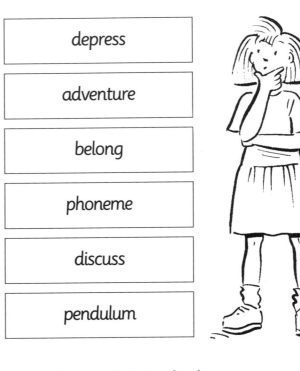

◆ Write each common root in a box below. Sort the words into the boxes.

◆ Use dictionaries and word banks to find two more words for each box.

✦ Word root jigsaw ✦

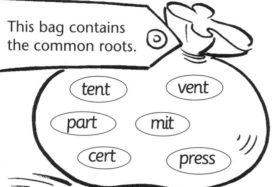

This bag contains the common roots.

tent   vent
part   mit
cert   press

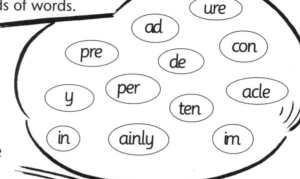

This bag contains beginnings and ends of words.

ad   ure
pre   de   con
y   per   acle
ten
in   ainly   im

✦ Choose a part from each bag to complete the jigsaw pieces.

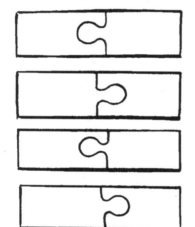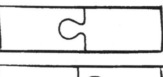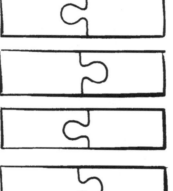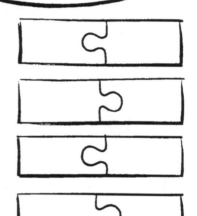

✦ Now sort the words into the boxes below. Add two more of your own. What is the common root?

The common root is _____

The common root is _____

The common root is _____

The common root is _____

The common root is _____

The common root is _____

Overall aims

- To explore spelling patterns of consonants.
- To investigate and formulate simple rules.
- To generate new words according to the rules and note exceptions.

Teacher information

- Children should develop fast and flexible word-attack skills, building upon previous phonemic knowledge. They should be investigating words and patterns in order to generate new words and formulate rules. Before they start this work, they should have revised distinguishing consonants from vowels.

 **LESSON ONE**

Intended learning

- To investigate the doubling of consonants at the ends of words when wordbuilding.
- To formulate rules from examples generated.

 Starting point: Whole class

- Use a poem such as *Out of School* by Hal Summers as a shared text. It contains lines such as: *There's a rising hum . . . a hop-scotch hop . . . a whirling top . . . a hair-pull and a slap . . .* Ask: What sort of noise is there? (Humming) What are the children doing? (Hopping and slapping) These words can be written down and the difference between the root word and the effect of word building (doubling the last letter of the root word) pointed out.
- Generate more examples – *rob, hot, dig* and wordbuild using *ed, ing, er*.
- Generalise, trying to find a rule. How many syllables are there in each of the words? What kind of letter is the final letter? What kind of letter is the preceding letter?
- What happens to words longer than one syllable? Give examples of words ending in *l* – *patrol, travel* – what happens when wordbuilding takes place?

 Group activities

- One group should take some of the single syllable words already provided and investigate what happens when they try to wordbuild. Devising a chart for class display could be useful.

word	a/the	I am	Yesterday I
run	runner	running	ran
skip	skipper	skipping	skipped

- Another group could find at least five single syllable words of their own and investigate what happens when they wordbuild. Are there any exceptions to the rule that was formulated?
- A further group could use reference sources in the classroom to find words of more than one syllable and investigate what happens when they wordbuild using *ed, ing* and *er*. They already have two examples from earlier. They could produce a similar chart to the other group for display and comparison.
- The most difficult assignment could concern a group of children investigating the *ll* sound at the end of words. What happens when it is a part of a single syllable word like ball, bell, pill? What happens to it in the suffix *full* and is there an impact on spelling, for example *playful, hopeful*? What about *skilful, beautiful*?

 Plenary session

Each group should present the work it has done to the class. Can the others add any other examples? Does the rule about wordbuilding onto single syllable words ending in a consonant work? What other single syllable words have been found? Does the rule work with words of more than one syllable? Exceptions should be noted. Keep the words displayed for the next session.

◆ LESSON TWO ◆

◆ Intended learning

- To identify the difference between soft and hard sounds in consonants.
- To generate a range of words containing such sounds.
- To formulate a rule concerning this and note any exceptions.

◆ Starting point: Whole class

- Revise the work of the previous lesson concerning doubling letters. Write up some examples of soft and hard *g* and *c* sounds, e.g. *pencil, coal, guitar, general*. Ask the children to read and pronounce them carefully noting the differences between sounds. They should be invited to come and circle the *c* and *g* letters and note the proximity of other letters, especially vowels. They could create a Carroll diagram to show where the sounds are found and what sort of sounds they are:

	hard	soft
sounds at beginning	guitar (next to *u*) coal (next to *o*)	general (next to *e*) city (next to *i*)
sounds in middle		pencil (next to *i*)

- Are there any rules the children can formulate about when *c* and *g* sounds are hard and soft and what combination of vowels and consonants create these sounds? Generate other words that follow the rules and write them on the Word Wall. Create silly sentences using such sounds, such as *Cats scream cream, Rice in a circle*, to illustrate the principle.

◆ Using the differentiated activity sheets

Activity sheet 1

This has been designed for children who need to distinguish between hard and soft consonant sounds.

Activity sheet 2

This aims to help raise children's awareness that wordbuilding using suffixes beginning with a consonant can lead to changing spelling.

Activity sheet 3

This is more difficult, in that it asks children to generate a rule for doubling consonants at the ends of words when wordbuilding.

◆ Plenary session

For Activity sheet 1

This group can share the categorisation of the soft and hard sounds and explain how they reached their choice. Are there rules that can be developed?

For Activity sheet 2

This group can explain what they have discovered about adding *ll* to words and whether there is a rule which could help the class. Any more words could be added to the Word Wall.

For Activity sheet 3

This group can present their findings about doubling consonants at the ends of words. The rule should be explained clearly and mediated by the teacher with examples at all stages – a single-syllable word, a consonant at the end of a word, a single vowel before the final consonant, adding *er*, *ing* and *ed*.

Present all the rules and ensure they are displayed in the class for future reference.

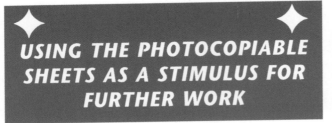

USING THE PHOTOCOPIABLE SHEETS AS A STIMULUS FOR FURTHER WORK

 Activity sheet 1

To reinforce this work, the children could:

✦ say the words to their partners and ask them to identify the type of sound;
✦ say five examples of hard and soft sounds to a partner and ask them to identify a rule to determine hard or soft sounds of that consonant;
✦ use the words as cards to play hard/soft matching games like *Snap*.

 Activity sheet 2

To develop further work, the children could:

✦ use simple one syllable words as starting points for rhyming by analogy – *fall, ball, small*;
✦ write these words down and use them as matching cards – does *bell* match with *ball*?
✦ use *full* as a word by itself in a sentence – *I am full of hate* – and then ask someone to use it as a suffix – *I am hateful*. The partner must spell the word correctly and note what has happened.

✦ Activity sheet 3

To extend this work, the children could:

✦ use single syllable words to match with endings and note changes in spelling – *rob + er* will need the final b to be doubled for *robber*.
✦ distinguish single-syllable words from two-syllable words by splitting the words at appropriate places. Do the same rules apply to both kinds of word?
✦ add *ly* to the end of words ending in *l* and other words and note differences – *careful* (note the word is more than one syllable and ends in single *l*) changes to *carefully*; *slow* (note the word ends in a *w*) changes to *slowly* – no change.

OTHER IDEAS FOR SPELLING PATTERNS FOR CONSONANTS

✦ Revise tenses of verbs using examples from this unit, referring particularly to changes that occur in spelling and also to peculiarities that need to be learned – *begin, beginning, began, begun*.

✦ Breaking down words into their constituent parts involves looking at the roots of words and this can often help us to learn to spell words. For example, *compete* (with an *e*) is the root of *competition*. Encourage children to look for the roots of words.

✦ Experiment with a talking word processor to see how sounds in words can be influenced by adding or removing letters, such as *ll, nn, tin* and *tion*.

✦ For proofreading practice, give the children words followed by their shapes. They should be able to see if the shape in terms of ascenders and descenders is correct or if the word is too long or short. The children are making judgements based on visual discrimination, not sound.

✦ Such word games can be made into puzzle books for when they are finding difficulty with particular endings. For example, there might be a series of activities on words with *ll* or *l* as endings or single-syllable words with doubled consonants in the middle, devised by the children with answers at the back. An editorial team should be formed who should discuss the needs of the reader and how they can make the book enjoyable and easy to access for him or her.

Name _____

◆ Soft and hard consonants ◆

◆ Read these words. Which are hard sounds? Which are soft sounds? Underline the sounds. Write **h** or **s** in the box.

g and *c*

gymnasium ☐

centre ☐

guitar ☐

circle ☐

guess ☐

except ☐

coal ☐

concert ☐

tongue ☐

great ☐

rice ☐

disguise ☐

general ☐

France ☐

cycle ☐

plague ☐

class ☐

city ☐

gold ☐

Cyprus ☐

cat ☐

cell ☐

pencil ☐

◆ So? Can you write some rules about when sounds are hard or soft?

soft c . . . when	soft g . . . when
hard g . . . when	**hard c . . . when**

Developing literacy Skills

Name _____

ll or l?

✦ Complete the chart by rhyming with words ending in **ll**.

ball	bell	fill	doll	dull	pull
fall	shell	pill			

✦ How many syllables do these words have? Can you make a rule about words ending with **ll**? _____

_____

✦ What happens when you want to add **full** as a suffix?

> I feel full of hope.
> I feel hopeful.

✦ Make some new words.

play → _playful_____

thank _____

skill _____

hate _____

spite _____

cheer _____

awe _____

tear _____

spoon _____

hand _____

beauty _____

✦ How many syllables do these words have? Can you make a rule about adding full as a suffix?

_____

_____

_____

✦ What exceptions have you found?

_____

_____

_____

©Hopscotch Educational Publishing

✦ Double the final consonant ✦

✦ Add **ing**, **er** and **ed** to these words, if possible. Check your answers.

	ing	er	ed

rob
hot
swim
dig
hop
skip
hum
fail
cool
wheel
feel

ing

er

ed

swimming   swimmer   ✗

✦ What do you notice? How many syllables do these have? What is the last letter? What are the letters before the final letter?

✦ Can you develop a rule? _____

_____

✦ Try doing the same with these words: pedal, expel, travel, patrol, shovel, marvel.

Homographs and homophones

 Overall aims

- To investigate and collect examples of homographs and homophones.
- To spell and use them in own writing.
- To reinforce knowledge of alternative phoneme spellings and generate own examples.

 Teacher information

- This work needs to be linked with earlier work on 'same phonemes, different spellings'.
- Homophones are words with common pronunciations but whose spellings are different – *bear, bare*. Homographs are words containing common letter strings but with different pronunciation – *bow* (to bow down low; a bow and arrow).

 **LESSON ONE**

 Intended learning

- To investigate and collect examples of homophones and homographs.
- To note differences between homophones and homographs.

 Starting point: Whole class

- An interesting starting point as a shared text would be an extract from *Alice in Wonderland*: the section entitled *A Long Tale*. Alice has had a conversation with the mouse which illustrates the confusions that can occur over homophones:
  "You promised to tell me your history, you know," said Alice . . .
  "Mine is a long and a sad tale!" said the mouse, turning to Alice and sighing.
  "It is a long tail, certainly," said Alice, looking down in wonder at the Mouse's tail; "but why do you call it sad?"
- Ask the children why the confusion arose. This is an example of a homophone. Can they think of

any more? Prompt them with such examples as *steel, stair, saw*. Ask them to come up and circle the letter strings making the vowel sound. What are the homophones? *(steal, stare, sore)* What are the letter strings making the vowel sounds now?

- Introducing homographs can be done using what children already know about word derivation: *homo* meaning the same, *phone* meaning sound, *graph* has to do with writing something down. Prompt the children with such words as *bow, read, wind*. Put them into sentences. Do they notice different pronunciations and meanings emerging? Can they generate any more examples? So, how are homophones different from homographs?

 **Group activities**

- One group should be given five words – *write, pair, there, road, fur* – and asked to find their homophones. (Encourage the use of dictionaries.)
- A second group should be given the task of finding at least five completely new words which have homophonic spellings.
- Another group should concentrate on some homographs supplied, but they should rhyme by analogy to find other words with similar spelling for both pronunciations.
- The most difficult task could be the challenge of finding at least four new homographs using whatever research facilities are available.

Plenary session

The first group should define homophones and present their examples. New words discovered by the second group can be tried out on the rest of the class. Homographs should also be listed and rhyming words discussed. What new words have been discovered? Challenge the rest of the group to put the words into sentences so they are sure of the context. Finally, ask children to distinguish between homophones and homographs and give an example of each.

Homographs and homophones

LESSON TWO

Intended learning

+ To revise work on homophones and homographs.
+ To reinforce knowledge of alternative phoneme spellings in own writing, for example with reference to pronouns.

Starting point: Whole class

+ Revise the work of the previous session.
+ Highlight common errors, such as confusion over *there/their*; *it's/its* and *were/we're*.
+ Show how pronouns replace nouns and that they can be of several types. Simple mistakes can be avoided by remembering: *their* is a possessive form, *there* is not (extend to *they're* being an abbreviated form of *they are*). Put these into sentences to see which sound correct – *They're (they are) clothes were dirty* is not correct. Also try this with *its* and *it's* (it is) – *The dog has hurt it's (it is) paw* cannot be correct.
+ Ask the children to give, in sentences, other examples of words that sound similar that can cause confusion.

◆ Using the differentiated activity sheets

Activity sheet 1

This has been designed so that the children can read, identify, spell and generate homophones.

Activity sheet 2

This aims to help children read homographs, noting different pronunciation and put them into a context. It also revises the idea of rhyming by analogy to generate new words.

Activity sheet 3

This is more difficult, in that it asks children to write about the pictures, paying attention to rules governing the spelling of pronouns. It also revises the use of apostrophes.

◆ Plenary session

For Activity sheet 1

Write matched homophones on the Word Wall and explain them. New homophones – words with three possible spellings – can be introduced and put into sentences by others.

For Activity sheet 2

The range of homographs can be introduced to the rest of the class and the idea that these do not just appear as single syllable words but also as 'words within words'. The rhyming equivalents can be discussed and categorised in chart form.

For Activity sheet 3

The third group can introduce their sentences written about the pictures and can explain how they know that the spellings of their 'difficult' words are correct, following the methods taught earlier in the lesson, ie can they put the words they have written into a different sentence context. Do they make sense then?

Homographs and homophones

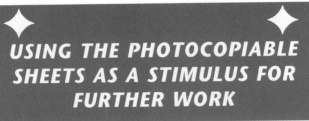

USING THE PHOTOCOPIABLE SHEETS AS A STIMULUS FOR FURTHER WORK

◆ Activity sheet 1

To reinforce work on homophones, children could:
- ◆ cut up cards and match homophones in a *Snap* game;
- ◆ give partners one card only and challenge them to find a homophone;
- ◆ give their partner a definition only, such as *the end of a dog's foot*, and ask them to find the appropriate word on a card (*paw*).

◆ Activity sheet 2

To further investigate homographs, children could:
- ◆ cut out the cards and match the words, but saying the sound that the word creates at the same time;
- ◆ challenge partners to put the word spoken into a sentence;
- ◆ blank out letters that make the sounds, and ask others to write them in, such as r _ _ gh, c _ _ gh.

◆ Activity sheet 3

To extend work on spelling problems to do with similar sounding words, children could:
- ◆ cut out pictures and ask each other questions about them, spelling out words such as *its/it's* when they come to them;
- ◆ cut out pictures and match with text to encourage careful reading;
- ◆ give one picture and a range of pronouns to a partner and ask them to develop a piece of writing. The pair should then go through the editing process together.

Generally, encourage the **Look, Say, Cover, Write, Say, Check** method for learning spellings. Keep in mind that there is a real relationship between handwriting and spelling.

OTHER IDEAS FOR HOMOGRAPHS AND HOMOPHONES

- ◆ Develop work on Greek prefixes and roots, using *homo, graph, phone* to generate more words, such as: What do telephone and geography mean?

- ◆ Groups of children could make word searches for others containing particular similar sounding words or words that are spelled the same but pronounced differently. These could be made into a book and used for all children. Discuss how such books are put together and internally organised – design, titles, contents pages – so others can easily find what they are looking for. This could even be made using a publishing program on a computer for a professional look.

- ◆ Sentence level work should be addressed concerning pronouns, their spelling and their use. For example, in independent writing what is the best way to vary the use of *he, she, the boy,* and so on?

- ◆ Give guidance and practice on using apostrophes, particularly for possession. A simple rule for possessive apostrophes is: turn the sentence around using **of** to stress the possessive and it always comes after the last letter, such as *the dogs tail*. Turn it around to find out what belongs to whom: *the tail of the dog*. The apostrophe will come after the last letter which is a *g* – hence *the dog's tail*. This method also explains to children why plurals are tricky, for example *two dogs tails –* the *tails of two dogs - s* is the last letter so the statement should read: *the two dogs' tails*.

- ◆ Many jokes rely on homophones. Children could collect them and make their own joke book for the class. They could add their own silly sentences to illustrate certain points. For example, *Where were they? We're where they were. They're not there now. Their house is where we were.*

Homophones

✦ Match the words that sound the same.

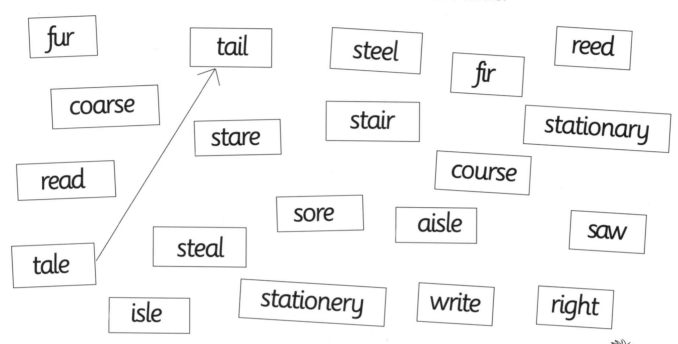

fur	tail	steel		reed
coarse			fir	
	stare	stair		stationary
read			course	
	sore	aisle		saw
tale	steal			
isle	stationery	write	right

✦ So, what do you think a homophone is? Write a definition.

_____

_____

✦ Now, match these homophones. Then find a third word that sounds the same but is spelled differently.

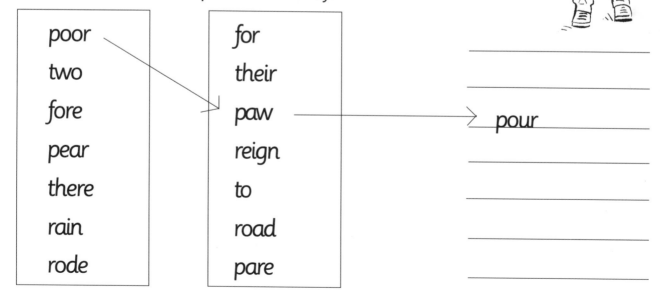

poor	for	
two	their	
fore	paw	pour _____
pear	reign	_____
there	to	_____
rain	road	_____
rode	pare	_____

Developing
literacy
Skills

Name _____

✦ Homographs ✦

✦ Circle the common letter strings. Write a word that rhymes. Make them sound different for each column. The first ones have been done for you.

f(oo)t	m(oo)n
c(ow)	b(ow)
rough	cough
through	bough
wind	kind
read	head
our	yours
thief	friend
nice	police

soot

now

shoot

so

✦ So, what do you think a homograph is? Write a definition.

_____

_____

✦ Now, turn over and write some of the words in sentences that explain their meanings.

Developing
literacy
Skills

◆ Confusing spellings ◆

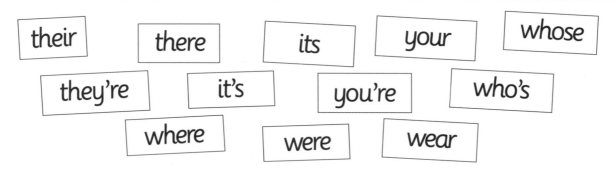

their	there	its	your	whose
they're	it's	you're	who's
where	were	wear

✦ Read the words above carefully. Write them in these columns according to their sounds. Circle the differences between them.

its it's				

✦ Use the words to write about these pictures.

It's a sunny day. _____

_____

_____

_____

continue on the back

Their tails are long. _____

_____

_____

_____

continue on the back

Spelling patterns for vowels

◆ Overall aims

◆ To identify and learn spellings of unstressed vowels in polysyllabic words.
◆ To analyse and apply spelling patterns for vowels.
◆ To generate own spelling rules about vowels from groups of words with similar patterns.
◆ To note and learn exceptions.

◆ Teacher information

◆ Children need to revise awareness of vowels and consonants, long and short vowel sounds, syllables, roots and suffixes before they can make the most from this section. Words that end in an *e* which are being given suffixes *ed, ing* and *y* will drop the *e*. This is a simple principle and the combination of letters created by the final *e* and the new vowel, will create a completely different sound. The famous *i* before *e* except after *c* rule needs to emerge from investigation, as there are many exceptions and application of the rule depends upon the *ee* sound in words.

◆ LESSON ONE ◆

◆ Intended learning

◆ To revise knowledge of vowels and consonants.
◆ To investigate what happens to words ending in *e* when word building takes place.
◆ To analyse and apply spelling patterns for vowels.
◆ To note and learn exceptions.
◆ To identify and learn spellings of unstressed vowels in polysyllabic words.

◆ Starting point: Whole class

◆ Revise the difference between vowels and consonants using alphabet charts.
◆ Introduce a text containing *ing* or *ed* endings to words, such as *The Cataract of Lodore* by Robert Southey, which describes the movement of a mountain stream and waterfall, and uses words such as *dripping* and *threading* and *shaking*.

◆ Write the words on the board. What do the children notice? They could come out and circle the endings that they notice. Others could underline the root of the word – the part of the word that comes before the ending. These can be categorised into complete words, such as *thread* and incomplete words, such as *shak* (the *e* is missing). They should be able to formulate a rule about wordbuilding onto words ending in vowels. Can they think of more examples?

◆ Group activities

◆ One group could produce a large chart to categorise complete word roots and incomplete roots after wordbuilding and produce rules to prove when it is necessary to drop the final *e*.
◆ A second group could be investigating the issue of when words end in *y*. Using dictionaries and IT sources they should collect together examples, such as *donkey, baby* and wordbuild to make plurals. Is there a rule concerning vowels?
◆ The most difficult task concerning polysyllabic words could be given to the most able. Give these children some of the words on Activity sheet 2 and ask them to investigate what they think the problem with spelling the words might be with reference to vowels. They should break the words into syllables for later use.

◆ Plenary session

One group could present their chart to the class, explaining the rules they have generated and write their words on the Word Wall. The second group should explain, using their examples, how vowels are affected in the plural. Rules should be explained and written for display. New examples should be generated. The final group can present their words and talk about what they have discovered. They could show that by breaking these words into syllables, there is a better chance of hearing the vowel sounds that are often missed out, such as *in – ter – est – ing*, not *in – tres – ting*.

 LESSON TWO

 Intended learning

- ✦ To identify and learn spellings of *ie/ei* words.
- ✦ To identify and learn spellings of unstressed vowels in polysyllabic words.
- ✦ To analyse and apply spelling rules for vowels.
- ✦ To generate own spelling rules.
- ✦ To note and learn exceptions.

✦ **Starting point: Whole class**

- ✦ Revise the work of the previous session, especially unstressed vowels, such as *description, interest, freedom, poisonous* and the help provided by breaking words into syllables for sounding out.
- ✦ Now ask children to think of words containing the *ee* sound. List and then categorise them:

ee	ea	ie	ei	e
sleep	pea	field	receive	me

- ✦ Concentrate on the *ie/ei* words as problem spellings.
- ✦ Generate lists of words using this phoneme. Can the children formulate a rule? What exceptions are there? After some of these have been found

you could write them a list which reads as a kind of rhythmical mnemonic:

> *seize, weird, heir, height, freight*
> *foreign, leisure, neither, neighbour*
> *counterfeit*

Chant this together a few times so the children can follow the words and hear them.

✦ **Using the differentiated activity sheets**

Activity sheet 1

This has been designed for children who need to concentrate on the rules concerning dropping the final *e* when wordbuilding.

Activity sheet 2

This is aimed at children who need to break down more difficult words into syllables and who can focus on vowels in words.

Activity sheet 3

This is aimed at those children who can categorise *ie/ei* words and can formulate rules and provide exceptions to the rule.

 Plenary session

Bring the whole class together to discuss their work.

For Activity sheet 1
These children could explain what happens when you add *ing* to words ending in *e* or *y*. Are there any exceptions to this rule?

For Activity sheet 2
These children need to explain why some vowels are problematic in words and how breaking words into syllables – this can be fun when pronouncing longer words – can help. Can they think of any more?

For Activity sheet 3
The *ie/ei* rule needs to be revised, but most importantly the exceptions to the rule need to be identified and strongly highlighted on the Word Wall. Chant the exceptions list again so the words are written and read in a memorable way by the children.

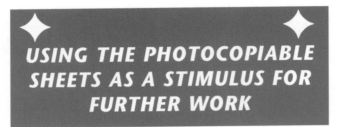

Spelling patterns for vowels

USING THE PHOTOCOPIABLE SHEETS AS A STIMULUS FOR FURTHER WORK

◆ Activity sheet 1

To consolidate and extend work on wordbuilding onto words ending in vowels, children could:

◆ use the cards containing the words to match with endings in order that children can spell out the new word correctly;

◆ show completed sheets to others and ask them from the evidence to formulate a spelling rule;

◆ match singular words ending in *y* with *ies* cards. What sound would *yies* make? Why, therefore, do such words not have this ending?

◆ Activity sheet 2

To investigate further unstressed vowels in polysyllabic words, children could:

◆ cut up the syllables and reassemble the words;

◆ block out the vowels in the words and ask children to write them in. They may have to use dictionaries;

◆ read out the words in an exaggerated way, stressing the separate vowels. Fun methods often aid memory.

◆ Activity sheet 3

To investigate rules concerning *ie/ei* spellings, children could:

◆ blank out *ie* or *ei* and ask others to write them back in. Check answers in a dictionary or from the Word Wall;

◆ in pairs, read each other words from the sheet and see if they can write the words in the correct columns;

◆ practice **Look, Say, Cover, Write, Say, Check**, using whatever method is appropriate to the learner, such as writing the letters in the air, inventing a mnemonic.

OTHER IDEAS FOR INVESTIGATING SPELLING PATTERNS FOR VOWELS

◆ Investigate how the sound of vowels can create a specific effect – long, round sounds as opposed to short sharp sounds. In independent writing children could try some of these effects out. 'Soup of the evening, beautiful soup . . .' by Lewis Carrol is a good example. Ask children to really exaggerate the vowel sounds to see how rich and long they are, giving an impression of thickness. Imagine they were swimming in chocolate; what words would they use to create the effect?

◆ Reference to syllables can also lead to useful work writing limericks which stress rhythm, stress and form. Children could find examples, analyse the structure of these poems, write their own and make anthologies for group reading.

◆ Haiku are also an effective poetic medium for counting syllables. David McCord summarises a haiku in haiku form:

Syllable writing,
Counting out your seventeen
Doesn't produce good poem.

◆ Use poetry to show how stressing words or parts of words in poetry can make a considerable difference. 'How they Brought the Good News from Ghent to Aix' by Browning makes maximum use of the rhythm of the words to create a galloping effect. Longfellow, in 'Hiawatha', uses the rhythm of the words very specifically to create the effect of the Native American drumming.

◆ The children could investigate words within words to learn to see if any vowel sounds are not being pronounced, and make lists of the words which are commonly misspelled.

Developing
literacy
Skills

✦ Vowels at the ends of words ✦

✦ Find some more examples of words ending in *e*. Show what happens when you add ***ing***. Write the correct spelling of the words.

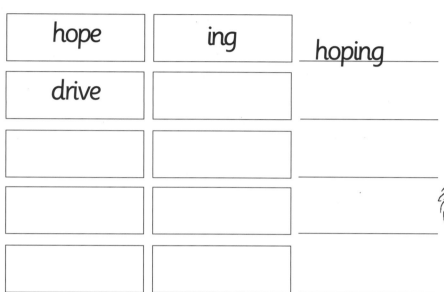

hope	ing	hoping
drive		

✦ What rule can you write about this?

_____

✦ What happens when a word ends in **y**? Do you always add **s**?
   Find some more examples. Show what happens.

baby	+ ies	babies		
donkey	+ s	_____		_____
	_____		_____

✦ What rule can you write about this?

_____

_____

◆ Unstressed vowels ◆

✦ Say the words. Which vowels do you think people miss out when they spell the words? Circle them.

company   portable   poisonous

interest   carpet

freedom   description   terrific

✦ Break the words into syllables. Write the word on the line. Circle the unstressed vowel.

			_____

			_____

com	pa	ny	comp(a)ny _____

			_____

			_____

			_____

			_____

Developing
Literacy
Skills

i before e?

✦ Read these words. Write them in the chart correctly.

deceive   friend   pier   relief   priest

thief   receive   conceit   chief

brief   siege   achieve   grief

deceit   ceiling   piece   company   receipt   conceive

ie	ei

✦ Find some more *ie* or *ei* words to add to your list.

✦ Can you find a rule by looking at the words? When is *ie* or *ei* used?

_____

_____

✦ You may have found a rule but there are a few exceptions. You will remember them if you learn to say this chant in rhythm.

"Seize, weird, heir, height, freight,
Foreign, leisure, neither, neighbour,
Counterfeit."

✦ Look up any words you do not understand.

 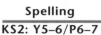

Spelling pronouns

Overall aims

- To collect examples of pronouns.
- To check and secure correct application of pronouns linked to grammar words.
- To read and spell pronouns related to context.
- To formulate and apply spelling rules for using pronouns.

Teacher information

- A pronoun is an item which replaces a noun or noun phrase in a sentence – *The cat ate the fish* becomes *It ate the fish* or *The cat ate it*, depending on the context of the text.
- There are five categories of pronouns: personal (*me, they*); possessive (*mine, his*); interrogative (*whose*); demonstrative (*those*); and relative (*who, whom*). Although it is not necessary for children to name them, it is important that they recognise that these different categories exist, and are able to sort pronouns into categories.
- The identification of possessive pronouns, such as *its, his, theirs*, is crucial if children are not going to splatter their writing with unnecessary apostrophes; as in *The cat ate its fish* indicates a possessive pronoun, while *It's eaten the fish* demonstrates a contraction of the verb phrase *It has.*

LESSON ONE

Intended learning

- To collect and classify examples of pronouns.
- To check and secure the correct application of pronouns linked to grammar work.

Starting point: Whole class

- Before starting work on pronouns, check and ensure that the children understand and can use the terms *noun* and *noun phrase* correctly. Then begin by indicating the need to recognise pronouns in a sentence by verbalising some

deliberately ambiguous statements, such as *Has Alev finished it yet? Is he here? Whose is this? I left mine at home.* Ask the children what the sentences might mean and why they are difficult to understand. Write the sentences on the board and ask the children to identify the problem areas and substitute other words. Give prompts such as *What hasn't Alev finished? What might I have left at home?* Explain that the words they have identified are called pronouns and that they replace nouns or noun phrases in a sentence.

Group activities

Divide the children into groups to work on the following activities. Explain that they will be looking for pronouns in different types of writing and exploring the kinds of nouns they replace. Depending on the time allotted for the session, the groups could rotate around the activities.

- Provide a group with a variety of ambiguous statements, such as *It's in the bag.* The children suggest and illustrate the possible missing nouns.
- Give another group a selection of pictures or advertisements from magazines, which include pronouns, such as *Our finest offer this year!* Identify the pronoun and what it is advertising.
- Use an extract from a known text. Ask the children to circle the pronouns in the text.

Plenary session

List the pronouns collected by the children and sort them into categories. Which sorts occurred most often? Try to provide examples for categories less well represented. Write a sentence on the board which includes a variety of nouns – *Tom took a penny to school to buy some sweets for Ms Smith.* Ask the children to replace one noun at a time with pronouns, until the sentence reads something like this – *He took it there to buy them for her!* Then replace the new pronouns with different nouns, finishing with something totally different, such as *Iqbal took the money to the shop to buy some samosas for Mum.*

◆ LESSON TWO ◆

✦ Intended learning

✦ To read and spell pronouns related to context.
✦ To formulate and apply spelling rules to using pronouns.

✦ Starting point: Whole class

✦ Revise the work from the previous lesson, reminding the children what they discovered about pronouns.
✦ The focus for the activities will be to explore personal pronouns, such as *me, him, they,* and possessive pronouns, such as *mine, his, theirs.* Ensure, by referring to the collections from the previous lesson, that the children recognise and understand the two categories.

✦ Using the differentiated activity sheets

Explain to the children that they will be exploring personal and possessive pronouns.

Activity sheet 1

This is aimed at children who can recognise nouns but need reinforcement to recognise the pronouns that often replace them.

Activity sheet 2

This is aimed at children who are able to recognise, sort and categorise personal and possessive pronouns, and now need further experience of using these in context.

Activity sheet 3

This is aimed at children who are able to recognise, sort and categorise personal and possessive pronouns, but may be experiencing confusion between possessive pronouns and the use of possessive apostrophes.

✦ Plenary session

Bring the whole class together to share and discuss the work. This time can be used to assess the understanding of each group, by prompting questions using familiar, enlarged texts containing examples of nouns and personal and possessive pronouns in context. Texts which contain lots of dialogue will be useful for identifying pronouns of these types.

For Activity sheet 1

Ask someone to identify and circle a noun in the extract. Ask "What pronoun would you replace it with?" Ask them to find an example of a possessive pronoun in the text. Prompt them to identify the character in the text to whom the pronoun is referring.

For Activity sheet 2

Use an enlarged, known text for a cloze procedure, making sure to leave enough nouns to keep the meaning clear. Read the text with one child filling in the gaps as the story progresses. Ask the children to identify the categories of pronouns found.

For Activity sheet 3

Give out various small objects to members of the class, including two or more objects for some children, and a few children sharing an object. Write one object on the board and ask the child to write who owns the object in a sentence, such as *Peter's bag is red.* Then ask someone to point and tell you whose bag is it, prompting the child to reply verbally using a pronoun, *his.* The child then writes the pronoun on the board.

As a closing activity, play a variation of Kim's Game. Ask several children to stand up holding their objects. One child studies the objects, before turning away. One or a pair of objects is removed. The child identifies the missing object by using a pronoun, *theirs, his, hers.*

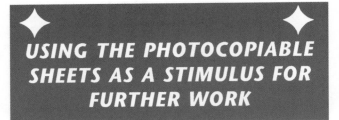

USING THE PHOTOCOPIABLE SHEETS AS A STIMULUS FOR FURTHER WORK

✦ Activity sheet 1

To consolidate their work on replacing nouns with pronouns, the children could:
✦ play Pronoun Snap or Pairs;
✦ invent a play that uses dialogue containing pronouns. Record the play on tape;
✦ explore the use of pronouns in advertising. They are usually addressed as if speaking to the reader directly, such as *Go on. Indulge yourself!* when advertising something naughty but nice! The children could create their own posters.

✦ Activity sheet 2

To consolidate their work on contextual use of pronouns and applying spelling rules, they could:
✦ collect and investigate homophones, such as *they're, their, there; who's, whose,* and generate rules of their own to explain the different usage, illustrating them with evidence from known texts;
✦ explore poems and rhymes, such as *Whose pigs are these?, Half-way up the stairs.*

✦ Activity sheet 3

To consolidate their work on identifying and spelling possessive pronouns, the children could:
✦ explore the use of possessive pronouns and possessive apostrophes in their own reading;
✦ investigate the historical development of possessive apostrophes. It derives from using a possessive pronoun, for example *John Brown his book* became *John Brown's book;*
✦ formulate rules to explain the use of apostrophes to indicate possession, and use these rules to support the use of apostrophes in their own writing.

OTHER IDEAS FOR EXPLORING PRONOUNS

✦ The work in this chapter has concentrated mainly on two types of pronouns. Explore the other categories through work on texts in Shared and Guided reading sessions, particularly focusing on play scripts and dialogue, which do not need to explicitly identify the subject.

✦ Questions and answers during investigative science work will generate examples of interrogative and demonstrative pronouns. This will help the children to structure their writing logically.

✦ Bear in mind that some languages do not have pronouns or do not distinguish between male and female, for example Bengali speaking children often use *he* and *she* indiscriminately when first learning English. Opportunities for speaking and listening activities, e.g. taped stories and plays which emphasise dialogue, should be provided to reinforce the written spelling activities.

✦ Generally, encourage the children to use the **Look, Say, Cover, Write, Say, Check** method for learning spellings.

Keep in mind that there is a real relationship between handwriting and spelling. Writing letter strings in a consistent and regular way helps children to register patterns in a multi-sensory way.

30
©Hopscotch Educational Publishing

Developing
literacy
Skills

Spelling
KS2: Y5–6/P6–7

✦ Who can they mean? ✦

the cat

Mr Smith

Mum

the goldfish

a tin

gloves

the children

✦ Do you know what the sentences below mean? Circle the pronouns in the sentences. Write the sentences again, using any of the nouns above, to make the meaning clearer.

She opened it and fed it.

_____

He left them on the bus.

_____

They saw it eat them!

_____

They lost them in school.

_____

It purred and she stroked it.

_____

They liked the food in it.

_____

✦ This present has lost its label. Now everyone thinks it's theirs. Change the personal pronoun to the possessive for each one.

 It's _____

 It's _____

It's _____

It's _____

 It's _____

It's _____

It's _____

✦ What do you notice about each possessive pronoun?

_____

31

✦ Personal and possessive pronouns ✦

✦ Match the pairs.

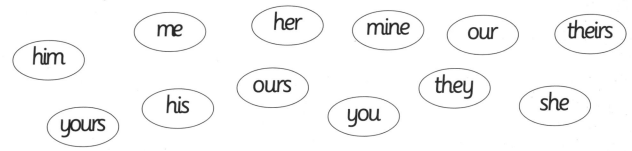

✦ Sort them into the two boxes.

personal	possessive

✦ Use the **possessive** pronouns from your collection to complete these sentences.

I've lost my pen. May I borrow _____ ?

Give Ann _____ book back!

Yum, jelly! Can I have _____ now?

The house next door to _____ is for sale.

Ask Sherrick and Sabia if this ball is _____ .

✦ Now write your own sentences using **personal** pronouns.

_____

_____

_____

✦ Can you write a rule about using personal and possessive pronouns?

✦ A pronoun challenge ✦

Mrs Green has lost her cat. Where can it be? She has asked the children to help her find it.

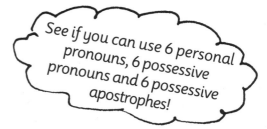
See if you can use 6 personal pronouns, 6 possessive pronouns and 6 possessive apostrophes!

✦ Write a play about what happens. Remember to write in the style of a playscript. Here are some characters and objects to include in your play.

Mrs Green

the children

Dad

the cat

flowers

a bowl

a hat

some sweets

a mouse

yourself!

✦ The first line of your play has been written for you.

Mrs Green: *Tabby, you naughty cat. Where are you?*

_____

_____

_____

_____

_____

_____

_____

(Continue your play on the back of this sheet.)

✦ Now, write the pronouns and possessive apostrophes you have used.

personal	possessive	possessive apostrophes

Transforming words

◆ Overall aims

- ◆ To investigate/classify examples of transforming words, such as changing tenses, making comparatives, changing verbs to nouns.
- ◆ To formulate and explore spelling rules for transforming words.
- ◆ To collect, read and spell families of words.
- ◆ To generate new words through transformation.

◆ Teacher information

- ◆ This chapter brings together much of the children's previous word experiences. The teacher will want to check, and revise where necessary, the use of the metalanguage needed, such as verbs, nouns, syllables, prefixes and suffixes, as well as the concepts of past and present tense, and first and third person writing. Revise and practise the rules that the children have generated and explored previously.
- ◆ It is important to stress the use of dictionaries, spellcheckers and word banks to establish understanding of word meaning and correct spelling, especially as children will be generating new, unfamiliar words. Good dictionaries are a rich source of the various transformations of a word, and children should be encouraged to explore adult dictionaries as well as children's ones.

◆ LESSON ONE ◆

◆ Intended learning

- ◆ To investigate and classify examples of transforming words.
- ◆ To formulate and explore spelling rules for transforming words.

◆ Starting point: Whole class

- ◆ Establish the children's understanding of the metalanguage required by revising previous work on nouns, verbs, prefixes, suffixes and root words. Refer to class word banks and dictionaries.

- ◆ Demonstrate transformation by using a word that has a variety of different forms, such as *play, player, playing, played, playful, playfulness, playground, display*. Ask the children to identify the changes. Discuss and categorise the types of changes made, such as prefixes added, tense changes.

◆ Group activities

Each group will be exploring a different type of transformation. The children should work on all the activities over time for experience across the range.

- ◆ **Verbs to nouns** – Give the children a variety of verbs on cards. Using dictionaries they find the matching noun, list and group them, formulating a rule to explain the transformation – for *educate, narrate, donate*, drop the *e* to become *education, narration, donation*.
- ◆ **Negation** – Provide three large pieces of paper, one headed *un*, the others *im* and *il*. Ask the children to find words that begin with these prefixes, list them, identify the root word and explain the transformation – *illegal, illogical, illiterate*. They will find some that are not transformations, such as *illness*. Prompt them to explain why this word is not included.
- ◆ **Comparatives** – Provide a chart listing the comparatives, *er, est and ish*. Challenge the children to collect a word for each column, seeing if they can find ones which stretch across all three, such as *big, bigger, biggest, biggish*. Explore rules for writing comparative words.

◆ Plenary session

Each group should report back. Encourage them to explain the rules they have formulated. As a closing activity, choose a root verb, such as *educate*. Each child in turn attempts to transform the word, such as *education, educator, educated, uneducated*. Repeat with a noun or an adjective, for example *kind, kindness, unkind, kinder, kindlier, mankind*.

Transforming words

◆LESSON TWO◆

◆ Intended learning

◆ To collect, read and spell families of words.
◆ To generate new words through transformation.

◆ Starting point: Whole class

◆ Revise the work from the previous lesson, reminding the children what they discovered about transforming words. Refer to the class collections and to the rules that the children formulated.

◆ Using the differentiated activity sheets

Explain to the children that they will be exploring families of words and ways in which they can be transformed. Remind them that they will be finding lots of new, unfamiliar words. They will need to refer to dictionaries to check the accuracy of their spelling and to find out what these new words mean.

Activity sheet 1

This is aimed at children who need to explore transforming verbs further, particularly tense changes.

Activity sheet 2

This is aimed at children who can identify root words and can recognise transformations, but need to generate and clarify the rules relating to the operations.

Activity sheet 3

This is aimed at children who have grasped the concepts of the various forms of transformation and need to explore these through generation of new words.

◆ Plenary session

For Activity sheet 1

Hold up a photograph from a newspaper. Ask the children to relate what is happening in the picture in one of the genres presented on the activity sheet. Identify one of the root words in one child's account. Ask that child to write the root word, transform it in the way it was spoken in the recount, and explain the changes made.

For Activity sheet 2

Ask a child to demonstrate on the board one example of a transformation machine from the activity sheet, and to explain the rules generated.

For Activity sheet 3

Show a card which displays a prefix or suffix from the activity sheet. Ask a child to write a series of transformations on the board. Ask for clarification and explanations of the changes made. Where appropriate, discuss word meaning.

As a closing activity, give out a set of challenge cards, such as *add ing, take away a suffix, add a prefix, change the verb to a noun*. Give a starter word, such as *unhelpful*. Children hold up their card if it can be used to transform the starter word. They write it on the board. Play continues on a word until no further transformations can be made.

Spelling
KS2: Y5–6/P6–7

Developing
literacy
Skills

©Hopscotch Educational Publishing

35

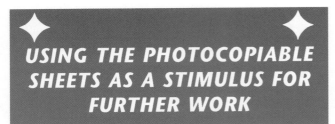

USING THE PHOTOCOPIABLE SHEETS AS A STIMULUS FOR FURTHER WORK

Activity sheet 1

Children could:
- read extracts from reports and recounts. Identify, sort and classify the tense changes;
- identify verbs in known stories and use them to create a game, transforming the word four times, for example *play, player, played, playing*. Consult word banks and class generated spelling rules for irregular verbs – *go, goes, going and went;*
- maintain own spelling logs to record and learn the spellings of verb tense changes.

Activity sheet 2

Children could:
- design their own transformation machines. Each part of the machine would need to identify the rule to be applied to make the next move;
- explore further the Transforming Sums activity. Extend this by giving the component parts a score and seeing if they can hit a target number;
- collect examples of transformed words from their own reading, classifying and learning them.

Activity sheet 3

Children could:
- make an attribute chart, choosing a word from their own reading, for example *donate*. They follow the chart down, answering yes or no, and writing the transformed word – *Can you change the tense? Yes – donated. Can you change it to a noun? Yes – donation. Can you use a comparative? No.*
- explore meanings of words, and the way the transformations affect the meanings, such as opposites – *happy* and *unhappy*, *-ology* added to a word meaning a science or a theory.

OTHER IDEAS FOR TRANSFORMING WORDS

- Provide activities to check understanding, for example Definition Pairs, with a set of words on one set of small cards and definitions on another.

- Play a version of Call My Bluff, asking three children to give a definition of a word, only one of which is right. Ask the class to identify reasons for their guesses based on their knowledge of word study. For example, "I know that any word with *un* at the beginning is a negation so *unproven* must mean that nobody really knows."

- Some words will not have immediately recognisable roots, such as *biology, telepathic*. This can lead to a study of word origins and the influences of other languages and cultures on the English language.

Generally, encourage the children to use the **Look, Say, Cover, Write, Say, Check** method for learning spellings.

Keep in mind that there is a real relationship between handwriting and spelling.

Writing letter strings in a consistent and regular way helps children to register patterns in a multi-sensory way.

◆ She won! ◆

◆ Write a commentary of this race as it nears the finishing line.

> And it's remarkable . . .

◆ Write a newspaper report for the next day's papers.

The Daily News

◆ Write what the girl said in the television interview.

> I am so pleased . . .

◆ Transformation machine ◆

◆ Write a different root word for the input box of each machine.
  Transform the word four times. Write what happens to your word as it
  passes through each part of the machine.

Developing
literacy
Skills

✦ Starting at the end! ✦

✦ You have been given 3 suffixes. Find 3 words that use this suffix.
Then for each word find 3 transformations.

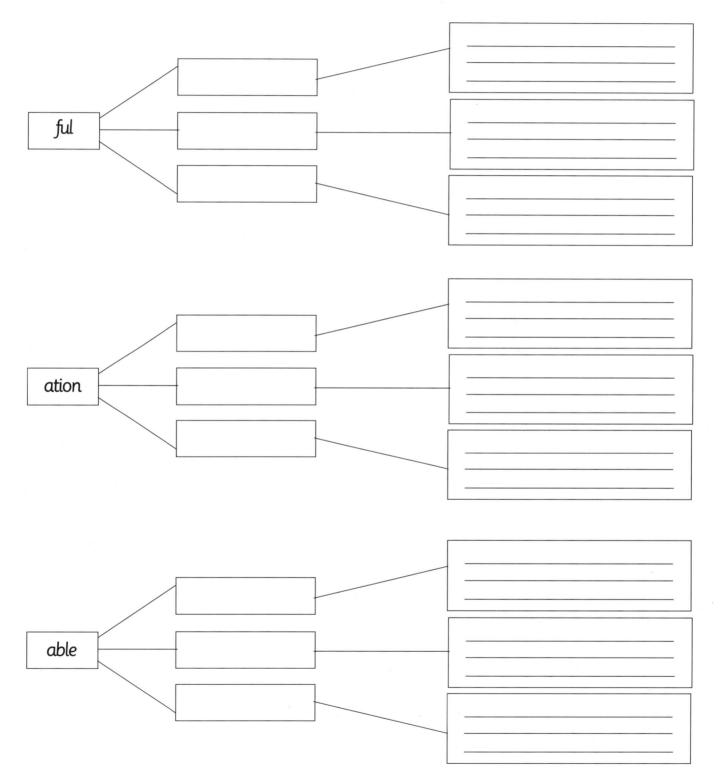

Derivation of words

 Overall aims

- To collect examples of word derivation through meanings.
- To investigate and compare word derivation through spelling patterns of stems using prefixes and suffixes.
- To spell and use words derived from parts of speech, and generate new words.

 Teacher information

- Children need to be aware that many parts of words have their own particular meanings and words are derived, or built up, from the building blocks of these meanings. Understanding this can help them to formulate rules and recognise patterns to assist in their word-attack skills.
- Suffixes, prefixes and roots of words all need to be revised and extended, so children can put together words and break them down into their constituent parts.
- When words are derived from other parts of speech, transformation occurs which can confuse children unless patterns are identified and rules defined through investigation.

 **◆ LESSON ONE ◆**

 Intended learning

- To collect examples through meanings of Greek and Latin prefixes.
- To generate new words using these prefixes using dictionaries.
- To investigate spelling patterns when using suffixes from Greek and Latin sources.

 Starting point: Whole class

- Display pictures of a bicycle, a tricycle, a triangle, triplets, a telephone and a telescope. Ask the children to name the objects and to write the words below the pictures. Can they identify any

parts of the words that repeat themselves or that the words appear to have in common? (*tri, tele* and *cycle*). Discuss what these parts of words might mean. *Cycle* is like circle, and the pictures have wheels in common, but how many? How many angles does a *triangle* have? How many children are in a set of *triplets*? The children should be able to work out the derivations.

- Explain that many words are made up of parts and these parts are called prefixes (before), suffixes (after) or root words, that most of the prefixes and suffixes are from Greek and Latin sources and are a result of the Roman invasion of Britain. Can the children think of any more *tri* words or *bi* words?
- This will be the opportunity to show children how to use an etymological dictionary.

 Group activities

- One group could find *bi*, *tri* and *tele* words that have to do with the meaning of the prefixes (two, three and far).
- Another group could be given three more new prefixes to investigate – *sub*, *photo* and *aqua* – and asked to collect and classify words they can find using them.
- A more confident group could be given complicated suffixes – *ology* and *graph*. They would have to make wider searches through dictionaries and IT sources to find words containing these suffixes and their meanings.

 Plenary session

Each group could explain to the class the words and meanings they have discovered. Add them to the display. Test the children to see if they can work out what words such as *submarine* mean, when they are told that *sub* means under. What could *marine* mean? What other words contain this? What is a *subway*? Consider *autograph* and *paragraph*. How can we find out the meanings of such suffixes?

 LESSON TWO

 Intended learning

✦ To revise work on prefixes and suffixes.
✦ To consider the roots of words and how roots can be changed to give new words.
✦ To generate words and rules resulting from transformations that may take place when words change from one part of speech to another or from a positive to a negative form.

 Starting point: Whole class

✦ Tell the children that they are going to magically transform words by adding just a few letters at the beginning (a prefix) to make the words negative. Give some examples – *appear, kind, visible, possible*. Ask the children to categorise the words – all *dis* words or all *in* words, for example. Now ask them to circle the prefix and underline the root word. Is there any change in spelling in both? The fact that when adding negative prefixes the root or the prefix does not change is an important spelling rule they should establish for themselves.

✦ Now ask them to look at suffixes and their impact on root words. Brainstorm verbs in categories, such as sport – *to run, to jump, to drive*. What happens when you change the form of the verb by adding a suffix such as *ed* and *ing*? Perform these transformations with the children (running, jumping, driving) but leave others for them to investigate in their group work.

 Using the differentiated activity sheets

Activity sheet 1

This provides an opportunity to collect and classify examples of words using Greek and Latin prefixes.

Activity sheet 2

This is aimed at those children who will gain from investigating spelling patterns using prefixes and suffixes from Greek and Latin sources.

Activity sheet 3

This involves generating words and rules resulting from transformations when words change from one part of speech to another or if they change from positive to negative. Dictionaries are essential.

✦ **Plenary session**

For Activity sheet 1

This group could explain what a prefix is and what they have learned about how they can change the meaning of a word. How did they find what the prefixes meant and what countries they came from? (Not just by looking in a dictionary but by finding examples and working out the meaning from those examples.) They could test this out on other members of the class.

For Activity sheet 2

This group could explain what a suffix is and how these – either Latin or Greek – can change the meaning of a word.

For Activity sheet 3

The third group will show what they have learned about adding to the beginning and the endings of root words and rules which they can formulate to help the rest of the class

---

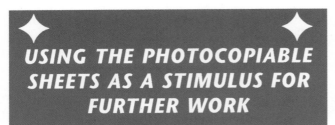

Derivation of words

USING THE PHOTOCOPIABLE SHEETS AS A STIMULUS FOR FURTHER WORK

◆ Activity sheet 1

- ✦ Use examples in the third column and challenge others to identify the prefix and to discover the meaning of it.
- ✦ Match the meanings to the prefixes and ask others to provide an example. Answers should be checked by using etymological dictionaries.
- ✦ Find other examples through work in history, maths or science which could be added to the list and categorised in the same way.

◆ Activity sheet 2

- ✦ Cut up the two parts of the words and match them correctly giving reasons.
- ✦ Cut up the parts and match them in different ways to create words – *geo* and *-graphy* (earth and writing combined).
- ✦ Start to add other suffixes to some of the words to change parts of speech – add *ist* to *geology* and *psychology* to make the people who work in this area. What spelling changes have to be made?

◆ Activity sheet 3

- ✦ Use words in the lists to identify parts of speech – is *a kingdom* a verb or a noun? It is *a* place (it has *a* in front of it so it must be a noun). Is there a verb to be made from the word?
- ✦ Make a game involving negatives to illustrate and reinforce the spelling rule – One person says, "I am kind". Another says, "No, you are the opposite, you are . . ." and has to spell the word correctly.
- ✦ Investigate what happens when you add endings to verbs or adjectives – adding *ing* or *able*. How many words have to change their endings? Consider *workable* and *changeable*.

OTHER IDEAS FOR USING THE DERIVATION OF WORDS

- ✦ Investigate different cultures' words for the same things, such as from the USA: *standing in line* (queue), *elevator* (lift), *gas* (petrol). Display language from different cultures who apparently speak the same language but use very different words. Which of these are now part of our language – *movie, fries*?

- ✦ Investigating slang is a good way to demonstrate how words are derived and this can be linked with history. The Elizabethan word for a highway robber was a *hugger-mugger*. What word today is derived from this? Victorian times provides a whole street language which can be investigated through adaptations of classics such as Oliver Twist or Victorian social historians such as Henry Mayhew. He identified mud-larks, the children who sifted through the Thames mud to find goods for sale, screevers were people who wrote letters for others, navvys dug the navigation canals.

- ✦ Display new words – those derived recently, such as *fax, Internet, trainer*. What is it that requires new words to be created? Where do new words come from? *Trainer* is from training shoe, once a sports shoe, now seen as a typical item of clothing. Such words need to be incorporated in and selected from their independent writing.

- ✦ Have a *dis* board, an *un* board and so on. Let children add to them as they find new examples. These form a useful resource for deciding upon rules, such as 'Do roots of words ever change when you add *dis*?'

©Hopscotch Educational Publishing

Spelling

◆ Prefixes ◆

Prefix	Meaning	Origin G or L	Examples
bi			(bi)cycle
tri			
tele	far away		
sub			(sub)marine
therm			
aqua			
auto			
photo			

✦ Suffixes from Greece ✦

✦ Look at the example. Find out what the parts of the word mean.
Write the word, then write a definition.

Greek for 'the Earth'

Greek suffix meaning 'subject of study'

| Ge | ology | _geology_ |

Definition: _____

| psych | ology | _____ |

Definition: _____

| auto | graph | _____ |

Definition: _____

| para | graph | _____ |

Definition: _____

| bureau | cracy | _____ |

Definition: _____

| demo | cracy | _____ |

Definition: _____

| claustro | phobia | _____ |

Definition: _____

| techno | phobia | _____ |

Definition: _____

Developing
literacy
Skills

✦ Changes in words ✦

✦ Complete the charts. Find your own examples.

Use a dictionary to help you.

Add: ship, ment, dom, ism

✳Adding a suffix can make a new <u>noun</u>.

From			To
King	(noun)	→→→→→→→→	kingdom
govern	(verb)	→→→→→→→→	
hero	(noun)	→→→→→→→→	
friend	(noun)	→→→→→→→→	

Add: able **or** ful. **Find some more.**

✳Adding a suffix can make new <u>adjectives</u>.

From		To
stress	→→→→→→→→→→	stressful
laugh	→→→→→→→→→→	
fashion	→→→→→→→→→→	

Add: ise, ing, ed. **Does the spelling change? Find some more.**

✳Adding a suffix can make new <u>verbs</u>.

From		To
crash	→→→→→→→→→→→→	crashed

Find some more examples.

✳Adding a negative prefix can make <u>opposites</u>.

dis +	un +	in/im/il +
dis appear	un kind	invisible

Developing
literacy
Skills

Our changing language

 Overall aims

- To collect and compare examples of language from other cultures, recognising that languages borrow from one another.
- To collect and investigate words that have come into English from other languages.
- To investigate how words and definitions have changed and continue to change and adapt.

 Teacher information

- Children should realise that language does not stand still. Yesterday's slang is today's Standard English. This can help them to understand why English spelling is sometimes so awkward.
- Each time England was invaded, a new language was introduced. So English now has a vocabulary of over 150,000 words – many times that of any other European language. This is why there are so many synonyms and spellings that break rules.

 **LESSON ONE**

 Intended learning

- To realise that English is a language made up of other languages.
- To realise that English is a changing language.
- To consider some reasons why English spelling is not regular.

Starting point: Whole class

- Introduce a short piece of 'historical' English – some Chaucer is useful, or a piece of contemporary writing from the period being studied in history. Challenge the children to read it. This can be great fun. Many will find that they can read and understand most of it after a while. Ask them which words they can identify and why and which words they cannot. They should point out these words and write them in separate lists for later research.

 Explain some of the words have fallen out of fashion and some have remained. This is a good example of language change. Discuss some historical reasons for this. When the Romans invaded what language did they speak? Did they learn to speak English or did they make others adopt their language?

 Group activities

- One group could look further at their history topic and any books in the classroom to find words that are not common today. They will need to check in dictionaries to find information on derivation.
- Another group could investigate the impact of 1066 by finding as many French words as possible in use today – in books, in signs, in the classroom – and try to formulate any rules about their spelling, such as the *et* ending in *ballet* is French. What sound do these letters normally make?
- An advanced group could attempt to rewrite the Chaucer or another historical passage in modern English. This will involve them finding meanings in etymological dictionaries.

Plenary session

- Bring the class together again to share ideas. The first group should explain the words they have found that relate to their history topic. Which words no longer exist? Why?

- Lists of French words could be brainstormed by the class and listed to see if the group's hypothesis is correct. Take *cabaret, ticket, buffet, chauffeur, dessert*. What makes a different sound? Is it because French is pronounced differently? Where did they look to find the meanings?

- The third group could read the historical passage and report back on what they have found. What spelling changes do they notice?

Spelling

KS2: Y5–6/P6–7

◆ LESSON TWO ◆

◆ Intended learning

◆ To investigate and collect words that have come into English from other cultures.
◆ To use etymological dictionaries.
◆ To investigate language change.

◆

Starting point: Whole class

◆ Revise the work from previous lesson.
◆ Provide a menu as a text, containing such words as *pizza, spaghetti, samosa, cola, chocolate*. Ask the children to read the words on the menu and point out the words that are easy to read and the ones where letter combinations seem strange (*zz* and *etti* are peculiar in English). Do the children know where these foods originally came from?
◆ Look at other words and explain their derivation. For example, *cola* comes from the African kola nut used as a flavouring. In an historical context chocolate is interesting. Aztecs used *chocalatl* to describe the unsweetened flavour of what we know as chocolate. It meant *bitter water*. Say the

ending many times to realise how awkward it is to pronounce – there are no endings similar in English. Laziness led to the softer *e* ending.
◆ Show the children the value of using an etymological dictionary. Investigate words that have changed meaning over the centuries.

◆ Using the differentiated activity sheets

Activity sheet 1

This is aimed at children who can use simple research techniques to collect and classify words.

Activity sheet 2

This is aimed at those children who can extend their investigations into word derivation and origins.

Activity sheet 3

This is aimed at a higher level, as it asks children to investigate and categorise words and definitions that have changed over time.

◆ Plenary session

For Activity sheet 1

This group could use a map of the world to point out where the words they have classified come from. They should explain how they found their answers and suggest how such words could have travelled to our culture. For example, Indian words from English colonialisation, American words from advertising and films.

For Activity sheet 2

This group could test the class on Anglo-Saxon terms. Can the words be better classified when they are heard or when they are seen written down? Where did they find the answers to their questions? This would also be a good way for children to identify the days of the week – the day of *Tiw* is obvious when heard, not so when read.

For Activity sheet 3

This group could explain the idea of words changing over time by using a word such as *wicked* or *mouse* which may mean different things to different children in the class. Others in the class could be given the older meanings to use in sentences.

Spelling

KS2: Y5–6/P6–7

Developing
literacy
Skills

©Hopscotch Educational Publishing

47

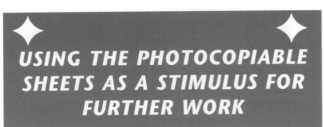

Our changing language

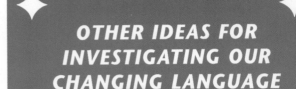

USING THE PHOTOCOPIABLE SHEETS AS A STIMULUS FOR FURTHER WORK

◆ Activity sheet 1

◆ Use word lists to create a quiz. For example, *safari comes from . . .* Let the children use dictionaries.
◆ Use the categorisation by country to collect more words – *banana* from Africa, *carnival* from Italy.
◆ Create a world languages game using a wall map and attached lists under each country. Which countries have provided English with most words?

◆ Activity sheet 2

◆ Match Anglo-Saxon words with their definitions, using sound only and then using the written form, noting which is the most difficult.
◆ As a part of a history topic, find new words to create a game – *cild* (child), *niht* (night), *cwen* (queen).
◆ In geography, make a further study of place names outside England. *Los Angeles* means the angels. Which country colonised this area?

◆ Activity sheet 3

◆ Use the word column sections as cards to challenge partners. What does this mean now? What might it have meant? Use a dictionary to check.
◆ Use the final column and the first column to match. Check answers in a dictionary.
◆ Research other words from reading pre-twentieth century books that have disappeared from usage or have changed meaning.

OTHER IDEAS FOR INVESTIGATING OUR CHANGING LANGUAGE

◆ Link with history topics to investigate words, such as *centurion*. How many other words can children find that use *cent*? What does it mean?

◆ In geography, consult large scale maps of the area to see if there has been an Anglo-Saxon or Viking influence, recognised by the use of place names.

◆ Children should look closely at their own surnames and trace their derivation. Is there a *Baker*? Is there a *Baxter*? This is derived from the term for a female baker. Some names served as simple addresses many hundreds of years ago. *River* and *Brook* marked where people lived. What does *Mac* dignify at the beginning of a name? What does *O'* mean? Challenge children to find these out and make a name book to explain derivations of children in the class. Do the same language rules about surname derivations apply to children whose families come from other countries?

◆ Do children's first names mean anything? Raymond is derived from the Latin *Rai mondo* – light of the world. Children could bring in books of names used for newborn babies to investigate meanings.

◆ Surveys could be carried out in school to find the most popular names in every year. Do they change? Is there a marked variance? If so, what does this depend on? Is it a television star, a football player?

48
©Hopscotch Educational Publishing

Spelling
KS2: Y5–6/P6–7

◆ World English ◆

◆ Find out which countries these words first came from.
   Write the words in the boxes.

zebra

pizza   supermarket   bazaar

Words from Italy	Words from India
Words from Africa	Words from America

cola

umbrella

gangster

bungalow

detergent

spaghetti   teenager   trek

                              piano

pyjamas   safari   pepper

◆ Find out where these words first came from:

kangaroo   judo   chocolate   maize

✦ Investigating Anglo-Saxon ✦

✦ Do you read 'Englisc'? This is what the Anglo-Saxons called their language.
On the lines, write what these words mean.

Do you want a drink?	waeter	_____
Can you read?	buc	_____
Wear it on your head.	haett	_____
Seven in a week.	daeg	_____
Not in front of you.	behindan	_____

So, has language changed that much?

✦ Anglo Saxons collected together names for the days of the week.
Match the day with its origin. Write it on the line.

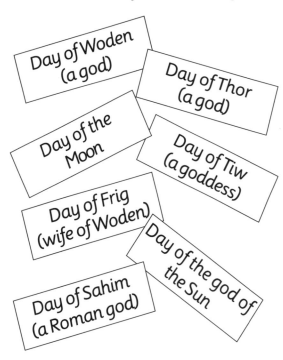

Monday _____

Tuesday _____

Wednesday _____

Thursday _____

Friday _____

Saturday _____

Sunday *Day of the God of the Sun*

✦ Did Anglo-Saxons live near you? Names of places tell us. Use maps to find some.

-ton meant a village; **-ham** meant an estate; **-burgh** meant a fort.

◆ Changing meanings ◆

Word	What it can mean today	What it could mean in the past
naughty	badly behaved	Shakespeare used the word to mean 'nothing' – an insult! ("Thou naughty nave")
wicked		
nice		precise
mouse		
humour		
vulgar		
villain		
meat		food

Words from other subjects

◆ Overall aims

◆ To collect and construct glossaries to define technical words derived from other subjects.
◆ To spell and use technical words derived from other subjects.
◆ To classify spelling patterns in technical words.
◆ To plot relationships in diagrams or charts.

◆ Teacher information

◆ Children often encounter unknown or unfamiliar words in texts. When reading and writing for information, they will need to bring clarity and understanding to the task. Familiarity with the roots, categories and origins of technical words will help them when encountering or generating new words in their work.
◆ The study of technical words should centre around real texts. Children need to see the words in context to identify purpose, and to be clear about the appropriate words for the genre in which they are writing.
◆ There should be a wide range of reading and writing for information going on in the classroom, enabling the children to base their studies around familiar texts.

◆ LESSON ONE ◆

◆ Intended learning

◆ To collect and construct glossaries to define technical words.

◆ Starting point: Whole class

◆ Refer the children to an information text with which they are familiar. Ask them to tell you what they know about the features of non-fiction books, encouraging them to list categories of subjects, styles and genre.
◆ Use an enlarged copy of an information text which contains a selection of specialist words, such as a book about the water cycle. Identify the subject of the book. Read it with the children. Identify and circle the technical words in the text, such as *evaporation, water vapour*. Ask the children for ideas for definitions of the words, based on their reading of the extract. Decide on the function or purpose of the words, and look at transformations of the words within the same text, such as *vapour, evaporates, evaporation*.

◆ Group activities

◆ Explain to the children that they will be looking at extracts from information books in the same way as the teaching example given.
◆ Give each group a passage from an information text to explore, providing each group with a different subject matter – geography or biology texts, instruction manuals, computer magazines. They should identify a collection of technical words, write a glossary definition, using the text as guidance (but not just copying the one in the book!), and explaining the function or purpose of the word in the text.

◆ Plenary session

Bring the whole class together for a plenary session. Each group reports back on the activities, shares the definitions they have written and puts the work on a working wall display.

As a closing activity play What's My Line? One child gives a word and a definition. The children guess what subject the word belongs to, giving reasons for choice. For example, "The word is geode and it means a cavity in a rock lined with crystals." The subject is geology. Same root identified.

52
©Hopscotch Educational Publishing

Developing
literacy
Skills

Spelling
KS2: Y5–6/P6–7

◆ LESSON TWO ◆

◆ Intended learning

◆ To spell and use technical words derived from other subjects.
◆ To classify spelling patterns in technical words.
◆ To plot relationships in diagrams or charts.

◆ Starting point: Whole class

◆ Revise the work from the previous lesson, reminding the children what they discovered about words which are derived from other subjects. Refer to the collections made.

◆ Using the differentiated activity sheets

You will need to provide a variety of information texts for reference, covering a variety of subjects, but with a least three books on each subject. Explain to the children that they will be collecting words from information texts, dictionaries and word banks. Point out that they will be looking for spelling patterns in the words they find, and that it is important to establish the meaning of the words they find.

Activity sheet 1

This is aimed at children who need guidance in order to identify patterns and sort according to categories.

Activity sheet 2

This is aimed at children who can identify technical words in text, but may need assistance in grouping these according to pattern.

Activity sheet 3

This is aimed at children who are able to identify technical words in text, and can categorise according to pattern, subject and function.

◆ Plenary session

For Activity sheet 1

Choose three familiar non-fiction texts, each on a different topic, and show these to the children. List at random two technical words from each of the books. Ask the children to identify which book the word would have come from, using the glossary if required. Ask them to think of another technical word for each subject.

For Activity sheet 2

Display a collection of books on different subjects. Invite children to come up and identify categories of words by asking questions such as, "Can you find me an example of a function word in each of the books?" and "Please find me a verb that is specific to each subject."

For Activity sheet 3

Write up a variety of technical words from a given subject area, such as *smelting, furnace, ore, molten*. Ask, "What do you know about each of these words?" Encourage the children to identify parts of words, functions and transformations. Ask, "Can you find a way to chart and record these words?". They may suggest gathering all the operational words together, or using a flow chart to order the words, for example: *ore – furnace – smelting – molten*.

As a closing activity, choose a word that the children may not have encountered previously. Ask them to predict possible meanings and to explain the reasons for their guesses. Look up the word together and find the real definition.

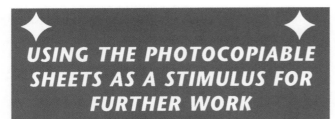

Words from other subjects

USING THE PHOTOCOPIABLE SHEETS AS A STIMULUS FOR FURTHER WORK

◆ Activity sheet 1

✦ Begin a display to which class members could contribute, for example *Technical words used in computer manuals. Can you add to our list?*

✦ Explore and display labelling and packaging, looking at contents lists, instructions, measures and so on.

✦ Keep a log of any computer error messages which may arise, such as *Working directory invalid,* and give a jargon-free explanation of what they mean.

◆ Activity sheet 2

✦ Explore writing in different genres, using writing frames as guidance if necessary. Highlight and record the technical words and the function they play in the text.

✦ Collect and categorise technical words from subject-specific magazines, such as *What PC?* or *What Hi Fi?*

✦ Collect technical words from at home related to the occupations or hobbies of parents and carers. Where possible arrange visits or demonstrations to see the words in action.

◆ Activity sheet 3

✦ Experiment with different ways of charting words – flow charts, venn diagrams, web diagrams – choosing the most appropriate way to explain relationships between words.

✦ Use a database to collect and classify words for different subjects or functions.

✦ Design and maintain class glossaries related to categories.

OTHER IDEAS FOR INVESTIGATING WORDS FROM OTHER SUBJECTS

✦ Technical words are specialised and do not have universal understanding. In any profession jargon develops as part of the job in hand, as anyone talking to a computer enthusiast will know! It is important that children recognise the specialist nature of the words they have been exploring and realise that they are often specific to a subject or situation, and therefore not appropriate to all contexts.

✦ Explore forms of writing which require specialised language, such as producing an instruction manual or writing a report. Emphasise the need for clarity of purpose and precise wording.

✦ Design and produce class or individual information books, bringing together the technical words for that subject and using them accurately. Produce glossaries to support the work.

✦ Continue to refer to the children's knowledge of metalanguage, and use this when generating new words by analogy or transformation.

54

©Hopscotch Educational Publishing

Developing
literacy
Skills

Spelling

KS2: Y5–6/P6–7

◆ What's the subject? ◆

◆ In the box below are some words that we relate to different subjects.
  Can you sort them out?

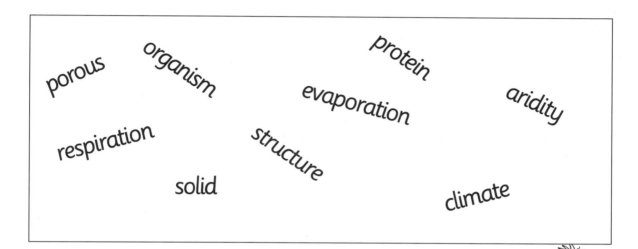

porous   organism   protein
                evaporation   aridity
respiration   structure
        solid   climate

◆ Write the words in the boxes below. Find three more words
  from each subject to add to the boxes.

Living things	Land	Materials

Spelling

KS2: Y5–6/P6–7

Developing
Literacy
Skills

Photocopiable

©Hopscotch Educational Publishing

55

Activity 2

◆ Subject words ◆

My subject is: [   ]

I looked in these books: 1 _____

2 _____

3 _____

I found these 10 subject words:

◆ Sort your words into categories. Explain first why you have sorted them in this way. Use the back of this sheet if you discover another category!

Words in this box:

_____

_____

_____

Words in this box:

_____

_____

_____

Words in this box:

_____

_____

_____

◆ Use the words you have found to write a glossary about your subject.

◆ Comparing subject words ◆

◆ Compare two books on the same subject. Find the technical words in the text. Decide on your own heading for each category. Find two words for each box and write a definition.

	Book 1 Title _____ _____	**Book 2** Title _____ _____
This box is for words that _____ _____ _____ _____	[ ] means _____ _____ [ ] means _____ _____	[ ] means _____ _____ [ ] means _____ _____
This box is for words that _____ _____ _____ _____	[ ] means _____ _____ [ ] means _____ _____	[ ] means _____ _____ [ ] means _____ _____
This box is for words that _____ _____ _____ _____	[ ] means _____ _____ [ ] means _____ _____	[ ] means _____ _____ [ ] means _____ _____

Overall aims

- To proofread and correct for misspelled words in their own (and others') writing.
- To keep personal spelling journals, using these to practise and learn new words.
- To develop strategies for spelling words.
- To invent and explore cryptic and coded definitions for words, using words within words and plays on words.

 Teacher information

- The development of children identifying and correcting their errors is a positive way forward. Correction of work by somebody else can often seem disheartening for a child who has worked hard on the content of a piece, but self-correction provides more ownership of the task.
- Establishing writing partners can be successful, but teachers need to ensure that the pairs are able to trust and support each other.
- Children who are proofreading their own work, and that of their writing partner, need to have an awareness of spelling rules and strategies. Encourage them to refer to class word banks, dictionaries and spellcheckers for support, and to employ strategies for identification of errors, such as Does it look right? Read what you've written – does that sound right ?

 LESSON ONE

 Intended learning

- To proofread and correct for misspelled words in their own (and others') writing.

Starting point: Whole class

- Show the children some draft writing of your own, with alterations and corrections. Discuss the purpose of the writing, emphasising that this was the first draft, and show them the finished version

as a comparison. Explain why you made changes and how you went about identifying errors – omission marks, crossings out, asterix for inclusions.
- Display an enlarged written text, preferably a child's, with that child's prior agreement. (It might be more useful to ask a child from another class to volunteer a piece of work). Read it with the class and together identify the errors. Devise class marking symbols for proofreading and correcting, to which everyone agrees. Display these for future reference.

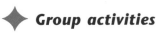 **Group activities**

- The children will be working in pairs on the following activity. You will need a variety of first drafts, some handwritten but also some type-written or word-processed texts which have typical typing errors, such as jumbled letters (*brian* for *brain*), double spaces or words without spaces in between.
- Give each pair a draft to work on and ask them to mark up the piece using the agreed class symbols to identify errors and make corrections. Encourage them to pay particular attention to types of errors which have not previously been identified. Note these and invent a marking code.

 Plenary session

Each group should report back on its activities. Identify new errors and add any new codes to the class chart. Some children may have invented different symbols for the same type of error. A class decision will need to be made as to which symbol is more appropriate or easier to use.

As a closing activity, write a line of text, including an error, on the board. Ask the children to identify the error and to mark it according to the agreed class symbols.

◆ LESSON TWO ◆

◆ Intended learning

◆ To keep personal spelling journals, using these to practise and learn new words, employing the **Look, Say, Cover, Write, Say, Check** strategy.
◆ To develop strategies for individually learning and spelling words.

◆ Starting point

◆ Revise the work from the previous lesson, reminding the children of their marking codes and the type of errors that they need to look for in their own writing.
◆ Identify words that you personally find tricky to spell, and ways in which you remind yourself. For example, saying **blanc-mange** as it is spelled not as it sounds, using the root as a guide as in *gratitude* and *grateful*. Remind the children also of the **Look, Say, Cover, Write, Say, Check** strategy.
◆ Brainstorm and list any ideas that the children may know already, such as using 'Never Eat Shredded Wheat' to recall the points of the compass.

Using the differentiated activity sheets

Explain to the children that they will be looking at ways to remember some tricky words of their own. Prompt them to look for and identify the problem parts of the words.

Activity sheet 1

This is aimed at children who may have difficulty retaining spellings and have problems with identifying errors in their own work.

Activity sheet 2

This is aimed at children who are able to identify errors in their own work, but find it difficult to retain the correct spelling.

Activity sheet 3

This is aimed at children who can identify errors and need to establish connections between known and unknown words in spelling logs.

◆ Plenary session

For Activity sheet 1

Choose a word from the sheet or one that a child has identified. Ask the child to write it on the board. Ask, "What was your tricky bit in this word? What did you do that helped you to remember it?"

For Activity sheet 2

Look at the words collected on the children's activity sheets. Choose one of the words and ask the child to write it on the board. Ask, "What was your tricky bit in this word? What did you do to help you remember it?"

For Activity sheet 3

Ask one child to list one of the groups of words collected on the activity sheet. Ask, "Can you tell me why you've grouped these words together? What way have you devised to help you remember how to spell them?"

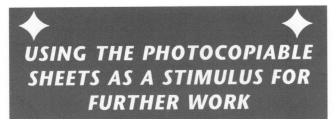

Strategies for spelling

USING THE PHOTOCOPIABLE SHEETS AS A STIMULUS FOR FURTHER WORK

Activity sheet 1

- ✦ Devise and display mnemonics that can be used by the whole class (Big Elephants Can't Add Up Sums Easily). Illustrations help the retention of these mnemonics.
- ✦ Investigate the position of letters on the computer keyboard. Look at *were, was, look*. Explore patterns, such as words that use the top line only (*top, try, pout*). Who can make the longest word? Practise typing the words as quickly as possible.
- ✦ Collect and record their own problematic words. Devise mnemonics for these. Frequently revisit and see if the words are now memorised.

Activity sheet 2

- ✦ Explore editorial proofreading marks. Obtain some contact sheets from publishers which demonstrate how these are used in practice.
- ✦ Investigate errors in a spellchecker. Look at the options provided and identify the problem areas of the words.
- ✦ Collect and record problematic words. Devise mnemonics for these. Frequently revisit and see if the words are now memorised.

Activity sheet 3

- ✦ Collect families of words and chart the connections using a web diagram or flow chart.
- ✦ Establish an editorial office in the classroom, with dictionaries, first drafts, proofs, and so on. Encourage editorial meetings, possibly with the children taking it in turns to be editor-in-chief! This could be developed into a class magazine or newspaper office.

OTHER IDEAS FOR DEVELOPING STRATEGIES FOR SPELLING

Riddles

- ✦ Read the children some examples of riddles, for example from *The Hobbit*. In a shared writing activity, devise riddles that would help them to spell words through analogy or transformation. They could then create some of their own.

Rhymes

- ✦ Read the children a simple text that uses rhyming, for example *bear* and *where*. Ask them to write a book for younger children to read and discuss why rhyme is helpful to children who are just beginning to read.
- ✦ Investigate homophones – *where* and *wear*. Collect examples from reading, such as *The Long Long Tale* in *Alice in Wonderland*.

Mnemonics

- ✦ Devise class mnemonics for words which are commonly misspelled. Illustrate and display them.
- ✦ Look for smaller words in longer words and find a phrase or saying to describe them, for example: 'There is a **rat** in sepa**rat**e' and 'Your fri**end** I will be till the **end**'.

◆ Tricky words ◆

◆ Here are some tricky words.

because   Wednesday   interesting
many   friend   February

◆ Use **Look, Say, Cover, Write, Say, Check** to write the words on the lines in these boxes.

◆ Design and illustrate a mnemonic to help you to spot the tricky bit and spell the word.

_____	_____

_____	_____

_____	_____

◆ Now choose some of your own tricky words.
Write and illustrate mnemonics for them.

✦ Mnemonics ✦

✦ With a friend, look through some writing you have done. Find 6 errors in your work. Write them correctly in this box.

✦ Design and illustrate a mnemonic for each to help you to remember the words in future.

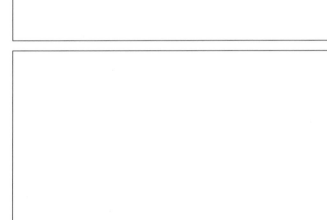

◆ What is the connection? ◆

◆ With a friend, look through some writing you have done.
   Find 6 errors in your work. Write the words correctly in this box.

◆ Write the words in these boxes and add three more to each box that
   have a similar spelling pattern or spelling rule. Write the connection.

My word is:	My word is:	My word is:
3 similar words are:	3 similar words are:	3 similar words are:
The connection is:	The connection is:	The connection is:

My word is:	My word is:	My word is:
3 similar words are:	3 similar words are:	3 similar words are:
The connection is:	The connection is:	The connection is:

A dreadful language?

I take it you already know
Of tough and bough and cough and dough?
Others may stumble, but not you
On hiccough, thorough, laugh and through.
Well done! And now you wish, perhaps,
To learn of less familiar traps?

Beware of heard, a dreadful word
That looks like beard and sounds like bird.
And dead: it's said like bed, not bead –
For goodness sake, don't call it 'deed'!
Watch out for meat and great and threat,
They rhyme with suite and straight and debt.

A moth is not a moth in mother
Nor both in bother, broth in brother.
And here is not a match for there
Nor dear and fear for bear and pear.
And then there's dose and rose and lose –
Just look them up – and goose and choose.

And cork and word and card and ward,
And font and front and word and sword,
And do and go and thwart and cart –
Come, come I've hardly made a start!
A dreadful language? Man alive,
I'd mastered it when I was five.

Hints for pronunciation for foreigners by T.S.W

©Hopscotch Educational Publishing